Bomford, Liz
  Hedgehogs.—(Nature in close up)
  I. Hedgehogs.—Juvenile literature
  I. Title   II. Series.
  599.3'3   QL737.I53

ISBN 0-7136-2728-X

Published by A & C Black (Publishers) Limited
35 Bedford Row, London WC1R 4JH

First published 1986
© 1986 Liz Bomford

ISBN 0-7136-2728-X

Filmset by August Filmsetting, Haydock, St Helens.
Colour origination by Hong Kong Graphic Arts Ltd.
Printed in Singapore by Tien Wah Press (Pte) Ltd.

Nature in Close-up

HEDGEHOGS

Liz Bomford

A & C Black · London

Contents

Introduction

You won't find many hedgehogs about during the day. They are nocturnal animals which means that they are only active at night. During the day they sleep in nests tucked away under the roots of a tree or deep in the leaf litter of a dry ditch.

There is only one kind of hedgehog in this country. It is called the European hedgehog. There are also Asiatic and African hedgehogs. Some of these hedgehogs have fur instead of prickles.

This book will tell you how the European hedgehog lives, what it eats and how it breeds. You can also find out how hedgehogs survive during the cold wintertime.

3

In close-up

The first thing that you notice when you find a hedgehog is that it is a prickly animal. The spines are really very stiff hairs. Each creamy-coloured spine has a brown band near the pointed end.

A hedgehog has several thousand spines, though older hedgehogs have more spines than young ones. Hedgehogs don't moult their spines each year, but the spines may break or get worn with age.

▲ Usually the hedgehog's spines lie flat

▲ When it is frightened, the hedgehog raises its spines for protection

4

Grooming is very difficult for hedgehogs, so amongst the prickles there are usually several hundred fleas. Don't worry, these fleas are special hedgehog fleas and they can't live on people.

Hedgehogs belong to the same group of animals as moles and shrews. They have small ears and a stumpy tail. Hedgehogs have quite long legs and they can run as fast as you can walk.

► All the fleas on this plate came from the hedgehog

▲ The hedgehog curls up using a special muscle

Keeping enemies away

Instead of running from an enemy, a hedgehog can use its spines to protect itself. The hedgehog will curl up tight, hiding its legs, head and soft belly in an armour of prickles. It can stay curled up like this for a long time without getting tired.

Hedgehogs do not have many serious enemies. Most animals that might eat them, such as foxes, badgers and polecats, cannot make the hedgehog uncurl. The enemy gets bored and goes away.

▼ The raised spines criss-cross in all directions

Excited young dogs may attack a hedgehog, but hedgehogs are not helpless. An angry hedgehog may jerk suddenly upwards, jamming its prickles into the dog's nose. This is very painful and the dog soon learns to leave hedgehogs alone. Some hedgehogs take advantage of their armour to steal food put out for pets.

When hedgehogs are frightened, they stand still, and raise their prickles. This is no defence against motor cars. Thousands of hedgehogs are killed each year on our roads, particularly in the springtime, when they have just woken from their winter sleep.

▶ This hedgehog is stealing the cats' supper

Many hedgehogs are killed on our roads at night ▶

7

What hedgehogs eat

Hedgehogs have bright, beady, eyes, but their sight is not very good. Snuffling around the garden, hedgehogs hunt for their food mainly by smell. They also have very good hearing. They can detect the tiny rustlings of insects scuttling under leaves.

Earthworms, beetles and caterpillars are the hedgehog's main food. After a shower of rain, the worms come up from the soil. But they will not come out if they think a bird or an animal is waiting. The hedgehog must tread softly to catch them.

▶ Earthworms are the hedgehog's main food

Hedgehogs are common in vegetable gardens where they can find plenty of slugs, snails and insect larvae to eat. These garden pests damage vegetables and so the hedgehog is a great help to gardeners.

Sometimes, hedgehogs eat pheasant or partridge eggs, as these birds make their nests on the ground. Young mice and voles are also eaten by hedgehogs.

► There are plenty of slugs on these cabbages

▼ The hedgehog can crack open a hen's egg with its large jaws

Rambling

During the night, the hedgehog wanders a long way in search of food. It has several nests scattered about to sleep in during the day.

You may find the footprints of a rambling hedgehog in soft mud near water. Hedgehogs can swim if necessary. A doggy-paddle will take them safely across a small pond or stream.

▲ The hedgehog snuffles through the grass searching for beetles

▼ Hedgehogs can swim if necessary

Wire fences are no barrier either, as hedgehogs can climb quite well. Coming down a steep slope the hedgehog's spines act as a useful cushion. The spines are springy, so when they are raised, the hedgehog can tumble off a high wall or roll down a bank without coming to any harm.

Hedgehogs are solitary animals which live and travel on their own. But at certain times of the year, they make longer journeys to look for a mate or to find better feeding grounds.

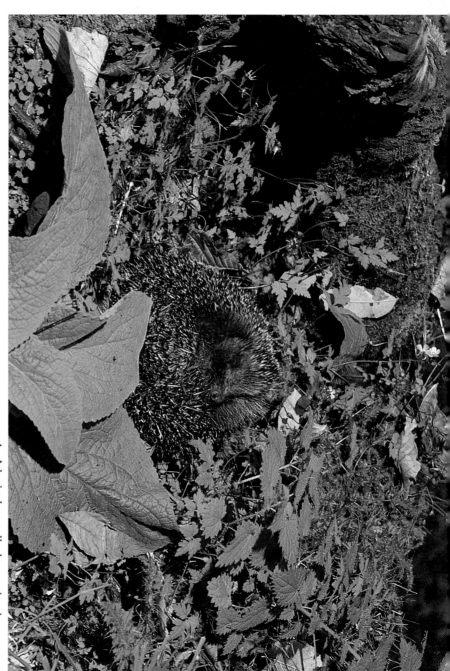

▶ A hedgehog rolls down a bank
without hurting itself

Sending signals

Hedgehogs have a strong smell. When they are on their travels, this smell warns other hedgehogs to keep away. Hedgehogs are not friendly towards each other and usually keep their distance. The strong smell is laced with chemical messages. Other hedgehogs can tell the sex and age of the traveller by its smell.

Certain tastes and smells make the hedgehog behave in a curious way. The hedgehog throws itself on to its side, frothing at the mouth. Then it tries to plaster its body with saliva. This behaviour is known as self-annointing. Young hedgehogs do it more often than adults, but no-one really knows why. However, hedgehog saliva is smelly and it may be that the young hedgehogs are trying to send a chemical message of their own.

▲ A young hedgehog self-annointing

▼ A cow sniffs at a curled up hedgeho[g]

12

When a female hedgehog is ready to mate her smell changes. Almost at once, hedgehogs for miles around pick up her scent and search for her.

▲ The male approaches cautiously

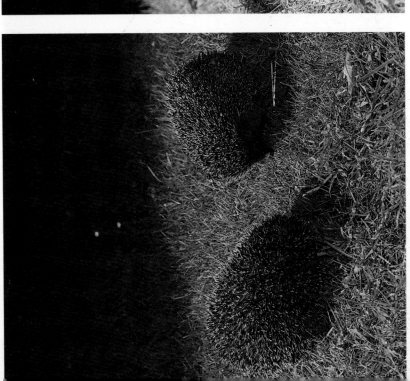

▲ Sometimes the circling lasts for several hours

Mating

Hedgehogs mate very carefully. Not only is the female armed with sharp prickles, but she is usually an unfriendly animal. The male hedgehog approaches her with caution.

At first, he walks round and round the female hedgehog making a snorting noise. The male hedgehog may circle the female for several hours. This courtship soothes the female hedgehog into lowering her spines.

▶ Eventually the female lowers her spines

Sometimes the female hedgehog's chemical message is picked up by other male hedgehogs in the area. They all wish to mate and so the first male must drive them away. His careful circling is interrupted by chases and scuffles with the other males.

The courtship can take so long that the female hedgehog becomes bored and wanders away. But sometimes one of the males persuades her to lower her spines so that he can mate with her.

The litter

After mating, the two hedgehogs separate. They will both live on their own again. In about five weeks, the female hedgehog will be ready to give birth to her litter of young hedgehogs.

About three weeks after the female hedgehog has mated, she looks for a safe place to make a maternity nest. This nest is larger and more comfortable than the usual overnight nest.

▼ The female hedgehog makes a maternity nest

Female hedgehogs have two litters each year. About five hedgehogs are usually born in the first litter, some time between May and July. Another litter arrives in September.

The young hedgehogs are born about five weeks after the female hedgehog has mated.

The young hedgehog's prickles are covered with white skin so that the mother is not injured as she gives birth. Their first prickles are white and begin to poke through the skin when the hedgehogs are a few hours old.

After a couple of days, a shock of dark spines with white tips emerge.

▶ A newborn hedgehog is covered with white skin

The first spines to poke through are white, then dark spines grow ▼

17

▲ 16-day old hedgehogs in the maternity nest

▼ The mother hedgehog suckles her two young

Growing up

Like many young animals, the hedgehogs are blind to begin with and quite helpless. They can't even roll up until they are eleven days old. Their eyes will open after fourteen days.

When the hedgehogs are about three weeks old, the mother takes them on short journeys away from the nest. To begin with, the mother suckles the young hedgehogs with her milk whenever they want food.

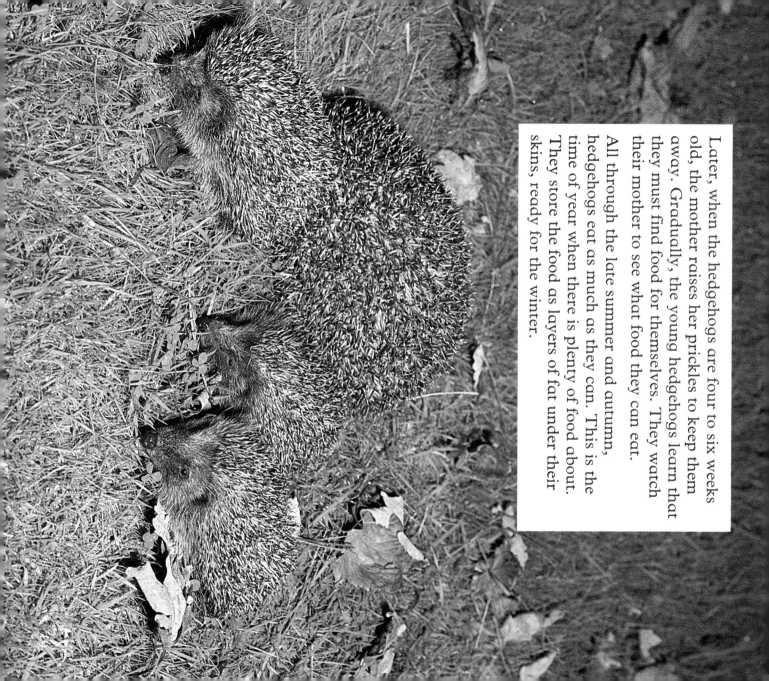

Later, when the hedgehogs are four to six weeks old, the mother raises her prickles to keep them away. Gradually, the young hedgehogs learn that they must find food for themselves. They watch their mother to see what food they can eat.

All through the late summer and autumn, hedgehogs eat as much as they can. This is the time of year when there is plenty of food about. They store the food as layers of fat under their skins, ready for the winter.

▲ The hedgehog needs dry grasses to make a hibernaculum

▼ Brambles help to keep enemies away

The hibernaculum

When the first cold weather comes, the hedgehog starts to look for a good place to build a winter nest. This nest is called a **hibernaculum,** and it is thicker than the summer nests. The hibernaculum is often made under a bramble bush. While the hedgehog is asleep, the bramble thorns help 20 protect it from enemies.

▲ The hedgehog combs the nest into shape with its prickles

After collecting a pile of dry grass and leaves, the hedgehog burrows into the middle of the pile to make its nest. With its prickles raised, the hedgehog combs the nest into shape by rolling round and round.

About the end of October, the hedgehog goes into a deep sleep called **hibernation.** Most animals sleep more during the cold winter months to save their energy, but this is not the same as true hibernation. While it sleeps, the hedgehog's temperature drops from 37°C to about 4.5 °C. Its heartbeat slows from 180 beats right down to about 20 beats per minute. This is just enough to keep the hibernating hedgehog alive.

Surviving the winter

The hedgehog's long winter sleep can last from October to March. During this hibernation, the layers of fat which the hedgehog put on during the summer months provide just enough energy to keep the hedgehog's body ticking over.

Hibernation is not always a continuous winter sleep. If the weather is warm, the hedgehog may wake up for a few hours to search for food. If the weather is very cold, the hedgehog may have to look for a warmer nest, perhaps in a compost heap in someone's garden.

▶ This starving hedgehog has woken up to search for food

A plate of pet-food could mean the difference between life and death ▼

Sometimes, young hedgehogs born late in the year don't have time to store enough fat to survive the winter. If you find a small hedgehog in your garden during cold weather, it may be starving, so do give it something to eat.

Try to find a dry corner, with a little hay or bedding, so that it can go back to sleep again. Remember not to lock the hedgehog in a shed. It may need to wake up and forage for food once more before the spring.

▲ The hedgehog turns over apples in search of insects

Hedgehog stories

There are lots of different myths and folk tales about hedgehogs. One old story, which may have come from a Greek legend, describes hedgehogs carrying fallen apples away from an orchard, stuck on their backs. Nowadays we know that hedgehogs seldom eat fruit and never store food. It is possible to stick an over-ripe apple on a hedgehogs's spines. But if you spot a hedgehog turning over windfall apples in an orchard, it is more likely to be looking for insects than trying to collect fruit.

Index